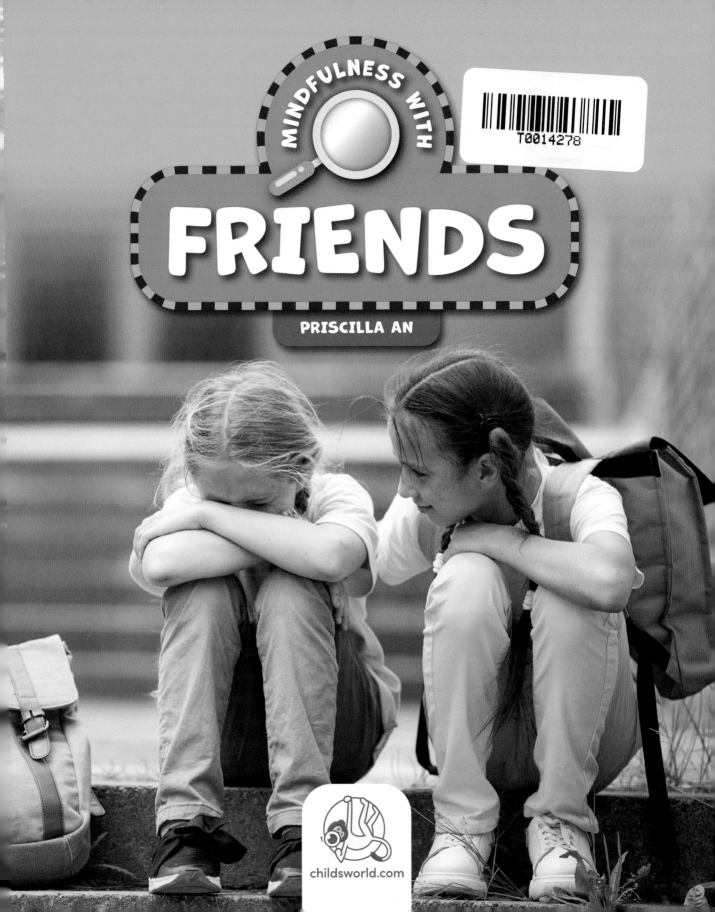

# MINDFULNESS WITH

# FRIENDS

PRISCILLA AN

childsworld.com

**The Child's World**
childsworld.com

**Published by The Child's World**
800-599-READ · www.childsworld.com

**Photography Credits**
Photographs ©: Shutterstock Images, cover, 1, 15, 16–17,
18, 20, 22; EZPhoto/Shutterstock Images, 3; Jacob Lund/
Shutterstock Images, 4–5; Yuriy Golub/Shutterstock
Images, 7, 8–9, 11, 12–13

**ISBN Information**
9781503869608 (Reinforced Library Binding)
9781503880955 (Portable Document Format)
9781503882263 (Online Multi-user eBook)
9781503883574 (Electronic Publication)
9781645498704 (Paperback)

**LCCN** 2022951200

**Printed in the United States of America**

Priscilla An is a children's book
editor and author. She lives in
Minnesota with her rabbit and
likes to practice mindfulness
through yoga.

# TABLE OF CONTENTS

# WHAT IS MINDFULNESS?

Friendships are not always easy. Sometimes friends can say hurtful things. It can be hard to know how to **comfort** a friend when he is feeling sad. Practicing mindfulness can help. Mindfulness is when people pay attention to their thoughts, feelings, and surroundings. Being mindful can help people think through their feelings. It can help people understand their friends' feelings, too.

Friendships take effort and time.

# SO MANY EMOTIONS

Danny and his best friend Lily are in robotics club together. They are working on robots for a competition next week. Danny is one of the speakers for the team. He does not feel ready. On top of feeling nervous, Danny is also **frustrated**. He had asked his mom if he could sleep over at another friend's house. His mom said no, and Danny could not understand why.

Robotics can help grow people's skills in science and technology.

Even good friends may fight sometimes.

Danny grumbles as he reaches to grab a piece for the robot. But Lily grabs the piece instead. "Why do you look so gloomy today?" she asks. Lily squints at him. "Your eyebrows are making the letter V," she laughs.

"Stop it," Danny says. He tries to pull the piece from Lily's hands. "Give it back!" Lily keeps holding it tightly. She is still laughing. She does not seem to notice that Danny is getting mad.

Danny feels something hot burning from his chest into his head. He feels like he is going to explode. "I said, *stop it*!" he screams at Lily. Lily drops the robot piece. "You are so annoying!" he tells her. Danny moves to another seat. Before he leaves, he sees Lily's eyes watering.

Danny tries to work on the robot. But he feels **distracted**. He did not mean to explode at Lily. It just happened!

Danny pauses. That was wrong. It did not "just happen." He closes his eyes. He tries to think about what went wrong.

Danny remembers that he was already feeling worried and frustrated before getting mad at Lily. When Lily grabbed the robot piece, Danny exploded. He took out his **negative** emotions on her. That did not solve anything. He still feels worried and upset. And on top of that, he now feels bad about how he treated Lily. It was not her fault he was in a bad mood.

Danny takes a deep breath. His emotions feel like knots in his stomach. He notices how that feels. Danny breathes out slowly. He thinks about what he can do. He decides to apologize.

## ANGER

Anger is one of the many emotions people feel. It is not a bad emotion. Sometimes anger can help people notice when something is not right. It can help protect people. But other times, anger can be damaging. When anger feels like it might explode, people can pause, take deep breaths, and think before acting.

People can try to think through their feelings before reacting.

Working together can be fun.

Danny walks over to Lily. Her eyes are red from crying. Danny is sad that his actions hurt his friend. He never wants to do that again. "I shouldn't have yelled at you," he says. "I was in a bad mood, but it was not OK to take it out on you. I'm sorry."

"Thank you," Lily says. "I'm glad you apologized to me."

"Can we work together on this robot?" Danny asks. "You're a great partner."

Lily nods. Danny is glad that Lily is his friend. The next time he feels worried or upset, he will pause before reacting. He will think through his feelings before they take over. Being mindful of his emotions helped him feel calmer. It helped him decide what to do next.

# CHAPTER 3

# MINDFUL LISTENING

After school ends, Bella and her friends meet outside. They have a group **presentation** for their science class. Today, they are practicing what to say. Everyone takes out their notes and their model planets. But before they start practicing, Sadie gets a phone call.

Sadie's face slowly turns pale. After the call ends, Sadie runs away from the group. It looks like she is crying.

"What do you think happened?" Owen whispers. "Sadie never cries."

Group projects can be more fun with friends.

Bella feels worried. She wants to go to Sadie and comfort her. But she is scared that Sadie will not like that. What if she wants to be alone?

"Bella," Bryce says, "I think you should check on Sadie. You're the closest to her."

"All right," Bella says. She still feels unsure. But it is better to try.

Bella sits next to Sadie. "Are you OK?" she asks.

Sadie lifts her head. "My grandma is in the hospital." She bursts into tears.

Bella pats her back. Sadie continues to talk about her grandma. Bella tries to listen, but she is busy thinking about what to say. Her mind slowly drifts away.

It may be hard to know what to say to a friend who is going through a hard time.

## WHAT IS EMPATHY?

Empathy is when people are able to see things from someone else's point of view. Even if a person has not experienced the same thing, she is able to share the other person's emotions. For example, when a friend is feeling sad, a person can feel sad with his friend. He can be with his friend and listen.

Listening is one of the best ways to comfort a friend.

"Bella, what do you think?" Sadie's voice breaks through Bella's thoughts. Bella feels bad. She did not hear anything her friend said.

"Sorry, I was not listening to you fully. Can you repeat what you said?" she asks.

This time, Bella tries to listen mindfully. Instead of thinking about what to say, Bella pays attention to Sadie's words. She leans forward and nods. She looks into Sadie's eyes. Bella notices when her mind starts to wander. When it does, she brings her attention back to Sadie.

After Sadie finishes talking, she hugs Bella. "Thanks for listening. It made me feel better."

Bella smiles at Sadie. "I'm always here for you." Bella is glad she listened mindfully to her friend. It helped her be more present for Sadie.

Bella thinks about how Sadie is feeling. If she were in Sadie's shoes, Bella would want to be home with her family. "You shouldn't be thinking of school right now. Can we walk you home? We can practice another time."

Sadie smiles. "That would be great."

Bryce and Owen had packed up the presentation materials. They join their friends. "We're here for you too, Sadie," Owen says.

"Let's get you home," Bryce adds.

"Thanks, guys," Sadie says.

As the four friends leave together, Bella makes a promise to herself. She will always listen and be there for her friends.

# WONDER MORE

### Wondering about New Information

How much did you know about mindfulness before reading this book? What new information did you learn? Write down two new facts that this book taught you. Was the new information surprising? Why or why not?

### Wondering How It Matters

What is one way being mindful with friends relates to your life? How do you think being mindful with friends relates to other kids' lives?

### Wondering Why

Mindful listening is an important tool to use with friends. Why do you think it is important to practice mindful listening? How might knowing this affect your life?

### Ways to Keep Wondering

Learning about mindfulness with friends can be a complex topic. After reading this book, what questions do you have about it? What can you do to learn more about mindfulness?

# HEAR: MINDFUL LISTENING

Listening is a good skill to practice. The next time you need to listen to a friend, try going through these steps.

1. **H**alt: Stop what you are doing and pay attention.

2. **E**njoy: Enjoy taking a deep breath to receive whatever your friend is saying.

3. **A**sk: Ask yourself if you are understanding what your friend is saying. If you did not understand, ask your friend to repeat what she said.

4. **R**eflect: Think about what you heard. Talk to your friend about what you heard. This shows that you were listening to your friend.

# GLOSSARY

**comfort** (KUHM-fert) To comfort someone is to give strength when the person feels sad or worried. Bella was able to comfort Sadie when she was feeling sad.

**damaging** (DA-muh-jing) Something damaging causes harm or injury to someone or something. Sometimes, anger can be damaging.

**distracted** (dih-STRAKT-ed) When people are distracted, they are not able to pay attention to a task. Danny was distracted by his thoughts when he tried to work on his robot.

**frustrated** (FRUH-stray-ted) To be frustrated is to be annoyed or angry. Danny was frustrated with his mom for not allowing him to sleep over at his friend's house.

**negative** (NEH-guh-tihv) Something negative is harmful and not helpful. Danny allowed his negative feelings to take over when he yelled at Lily.

**presentation** (preh-zen-TAY-shun) A presentation is when people are showing something to a group of people. Sadie and her friends were practicing for a science presentation.

# FIND OUT MORE

## In the Library

Anthony, William. *Mindfulness.*
Minneapolis, MN: Bearport, 2021.

Krekelberg, Alyssa. *We Need Each Other: Being a Good Friend.* Parker, CO: The Child's World, 2021.

Verde, Susan. *I Am Human: A Book of Empathy.* New York, NY: Abrams, 2018.

## On the Web

Visit our website for links about mindfulness with friends:
**childsworld.com/links**

*Note to Parents, Caregivers, Teachers, and Librarians: We routinely verify our Web links to make sure they are safe and active sites. So encourage your readers to check them out!*

# INDEX